FAIR TRADE FIRST

SARAH RIDLEY

W
FRANKLIN WATTS
LONDON·SYDNEY

This edition published in Great Britain in 2023
by Hodder & Stoughton
Copyright © Hodder & Stoughton, 2023
All rights reserved

Editor: Julia Bird
Design: Jim Green

HB ISBN 978 1 4451 7302 3
PB ISBN 978 1 4451 73030

Printed in Dubai

Picture credits:

Alamy: Joerg Boethling 34b, 36t; ETham 13t; Granger Historical Picture Archive 4t; Edward Jonkler 36b; PA Images 42t; Simon Rawles 31t, 32b, 34t,40tr, 41tr; Edd Westmacott 21b. **Balla Sport:** Thanks to Angus Coull 11br, 38t, 43t; Thanks to Irfan Smirza 38b. **Clipper Tea**: Simon Rawles 26b, 28t, 28b, 29. **Divine Chocolate:** 8t, 8b, 9tr, 10t, 13c, 43b; Kim Naylor 12b; Pete Patisson 9t; Dominique Fofanah/Fairtrade Foundation 14t, 14c, 15t, 15c,15b, 16t, 16b; Eduardo Martino/Fairtrade Foundation 23b. **Fairtrade Foundation:** 10bl, 22b, 24cl, 39t, 39l, 41b. **iStock:** Undefined undefined 26cl. **Nature PL:** Felicity Lanchester 11t. **Panos Pictures:** Edouardo Martino/Fairtrade Foundation 18t, 18b, 19t, 19b, 20t, 20b, 23t; Gary John Norman 30bl. **Eliza RidleyJohnson:** 25t. **Suzanne Lee:** 37t.**Shutterstock:** Africa Studio 26t; Alchemist from India 40bl; Aniok 34-35bg; Ataly 40tl; Bchyla 22c; Bergamont 6tl; Boonchuay 41tl; CRS Photo 35b, 36c; C sa bum 6tr; Epine 6bl, 18-19bg, 20c, 40br; Freedomnaruk 7tc; FuzzyLogicKate 10-11b, 13b,14-15bg, 16-17bg; HamsterMan 31b; Jerry Horbert 7tr; Ittipon 30t; Alenka Karabanova 4-5 bg, 42-43 bg; Svetlana Kononova 1, 2; Julian Lott 32t; Amy Ly 24tl, 24bc, 25b; Mailsonpignata 7bl; Mar2029 RSus 26-27bg; Erika J Mitchell 42b; Monkey Business Images 5t; Eliya Nuwara, Sri Lanka 27t; Oksana2010 33t; Byron Ortiz 24tr, 24bl; M Unal Ozmen 17b; Pandech 24bl; Suradech Prapairat 17t; RaiDztor 6-7; Iryna Rasko 27b; Real Window Creative 24br; Alf Ribero 5c, 5b, 35t; Alvaro Trabazo Rivas 35c; Alex Rockheart 7tl, 7bc, 22tc, 22b, 23cr; Sarot In-Orn 21t; Thinglass 19b; Visit Roemvanitch 22t; Valentyn Volkov 12t; e Wilding 4b; Xerography 30br, 32b.

Should there be any inadvertent omission, please apply to the publisher for rectification.

Many thanks to Joanna Milis and Claire Arnott at the Fairtrade Foundation and Tom Steele at Divine Chocolate for their help with this book.

Franklin Watts
An imprint of
Hachette Children's Group
Part of Hodder & Stoughton
Carmelite House
50 Victoria Embankment
London EC4Y 0DZ

An Hachette UK Company
www.hachette.co.uk
www.hachettechildrens.co.uk

MIX
Paper | Supporting responsible forestry
FSC® C104740

CONTENTS

- **4** Chapter 1: What is fair trade?
- **12** Chapter 2: A Fairtrade story: chocolate
- **18** Chapter 3: A Fairtrade story: bananas
- **22** Chapter 4: A Fairtrade story: coffee
- **26** Chapter 5: A Fairtrade story: tea
- **30** Chapter 6: A Fairtrade story: sugar
- **34** Chapter 7: A Fairtrade story: cotton
- **38** Chapter 8: More Fairtrade products
- **42** Chapter 9: Support Fairtrade
- **44** Questions and answers
- **46** Glossary and further information
- **48** Index

WHAT IS FAIR TRADE?

Have you ever traded cards with a friend? You have a card that your friend wants, and they have one that you want. By trading the cards, you both end up happy.

Stone axe heads like this one were traded across Europe from around 5,000 years ago.

Trading up

People have been trading goods with each other for thousands of years. Prehistoric people traded any extra food they had grown with others who had something they wanted, such as a stone tool. Today trade almost always involves using money to buy and sell the goods and services that we want or need.

Local vs. global

For a long time, people met together to trade food and goods in local markets, although some of these products might have been made, or grown, far away. Over time, trade has changed a lot. Now goods and services are traded all across the world.

This busy market in Hong Kong is full of people buying and selling food.

CHAPTER 1: WHAT IS FAIR TRADE?

What is a service?

A service is work that is done to help people. Teachers, for example, provide a service by teaching children and students. They are paid to provide this service. Other service industry jobs include being a banker, cleaner, rubbish collector or waiter.

A supply chain

Returning to trade, some of the foods or goods that we enjoy are grown or produced far away. To reach our shops, they pass along a chain of relationships called a supply chain. Take mangoes grown in Brazil.

The farmer harvests the mangoes when they are ready.

→ The farmer sells the mangoes to an agent.

→ The agent sells the mangoes to a wholesaler, who transports the mangoes around the world.

↓

The wholesaler sells the mangoes to a supermarket or shop.

← The shop sells some mangoes to its customers.

In this supply chain, the farmer, the agent, the wholesaler and the supermarket all need to make money from selling the mangoes.

5

1.
Colombia:
Bananas

2.
Peru:
Coffee cherries

1.
2.

IT ALL STARTS WITH THE PRODUCERS

Have you ever wondered where the things we eat and drink, and the materials for the things we wear, come from? Some of them are grown by farmers in your own country. Others are grown by farmers living in countries that are far away. Wherever they live, farmers are called producers.

Small-scale producers

This book is going to focus on some of the small-scale producers who grow the crops shown on this map. They live in less wealthy countries and grow their crops on small plots of land. Much of what they grow is sold to people in wealthier countries in Europe, Australasia and North America.

CHAPTER 1: WHAT IS FAIR TRADE?

3. Ghana/Sierra Leone: Cocoa beans

4. India: Cotton bolls and tea leaves

5. Malawi: Sugar cane

Money struggles

Many small-scale producers live in poverty. Just like every family, they need to pay for somewhere to live, buy food and clothes, and be able to send their children to school. Sadly, these farmers may have no control over the price they are paid and are often underpaid for their products. This can leave them struggling to pay for their basic needs.

7

MAKING TRADE FAIR

Many people believe that the producers who grow the products we buy should be able to make a decent living from their work, and not be pushed further into poverty. They want to see fairer trade terms for all. That's where the Fairtrade movement comes in.

Fairtrade changes lives

Take Kuapa Kokoo in Ghana. In the early 1990s, a few cocoa farmers joined together to form a co-operative. The farmers worked together to help each other during the farming year, and to bring their cocoa beans to market. Several organisations helped the farmers meet Fairtrade Standards (see right) and Kuapa Kokoo farmers started selling some of their cocoa beans on Fairtrade terms.

Farmers from the Kuapa Kokoo co-operative work together. Here they are turning the cocoa beans to help them dry.

CHAPTER 1: WHAT IS FAIR TRADE?

Kuapa Kokoo farmers have spent the Fairtrade Premium (see below) in many ways, including building new water pumps to provide clean, safe drinking water.

How does it work?

To be paid a Fairtrade price, Kuapa Kokoo and other Fairtrade producers must agree to certain rules called Fairtrade Standards. These include the need to:
- farm or work safely
- not harm the environment for future generations
- pay workers fairly and not employ children
- let everyone, including women, have a say in the running of the co-operative.

In return the Fairtrade producers receive:

- the Fairtrade Minimum Price – to cover the cost of growing the crop and enough money to survive
- the Fairtrade Premium – extra money paid to benefit the co-operative's community.

Kuapa Kokoo has helped many female cocoa farmers, including Ama, to grow their own cocoa to Fairtrade Standards.

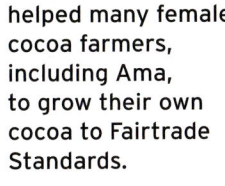

What is a 'fair' price?

A Fairtrade buyer will pay the producers in the co-operative at least the Fairtrade Minimum Price for their goods or harvest. This price should cover the cost of growing the crop without harming the environment, plus a little more. And if the world price for the goods, for instance cocoa beans, is higher than the Fairtrade Minimum Price, the buyer will pay that higher price for the beans.

9

FAIRTRADE IN ACTION

Organisations across the world work hard to help fair trade happen. Many of them are connected to Fairtrade International or the World Fair Trade Organization. Others are charities dedicated to bringing an end to poverty. They support farmers and workers to meet Fairtrade Standards and bring attention to the importance of fair trade. Over two million farmers and workers are now Fairtrade certified.

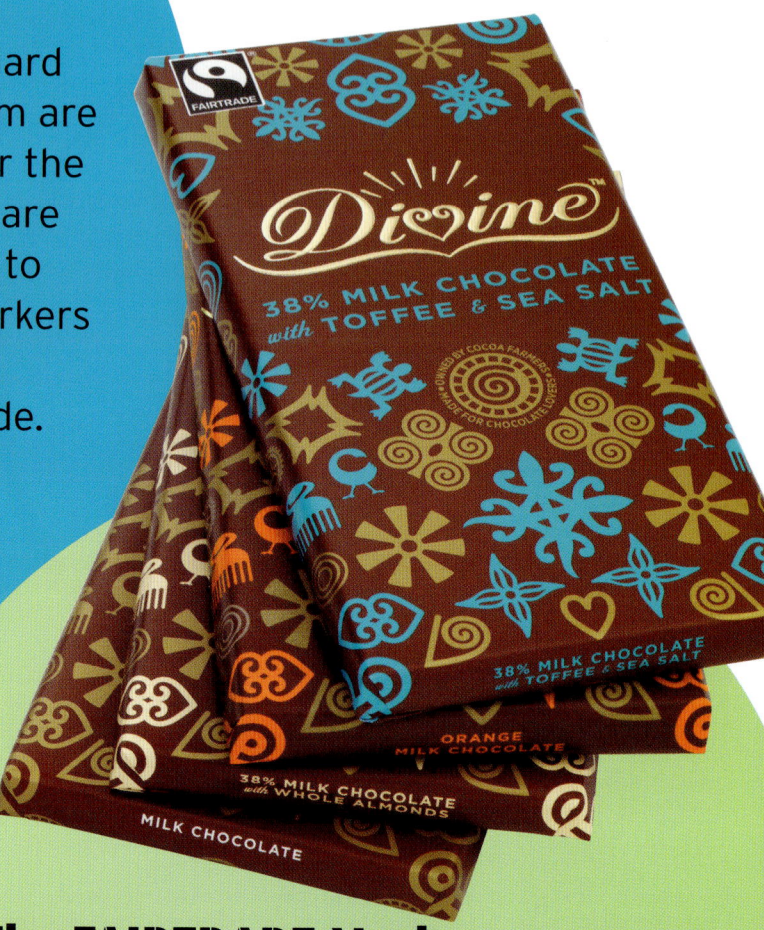

Support cocoa farmers by looking for the FAIRTRADE Mark on chocolate bars.

The FAIRTRADE Mark

Have you ever noticed the FAIRTRADE Mark on food packaging? It tells shoppers that a food or product is Fairtrade. Take a Fairtrade chocolate bar. The FAIRTRADE Mark tells you that the cocoa and sugar used to make the chocolate were bought from producers for a fair price. It also tells you that the farmers worked safely in ways that did not harm the natural world.

Here are a few different FAIRTRADE Marks that you might see on products.

CHAPTER 1: WHAT IS FAIR TRADE?

The Fairtrade Premium

Wherever you see the FAIRTRADE Mark, you know that the producers received a Fairtrade Premium (see page 9). This extra sum of money is paid by Fairtrade buyers to Fairtrade co-operatives each year, on top of at least the Fairtrade Minimum Price for the goods. Together, members of co-operatives decide how to spend this money to improve life in their community.

White-necked rockfowl

In Sierra Leone, the Fairtrade Premium has paid for training so that farmers learn how to farm without harming the local Gola rainforest and its wildlife, such as the white-necked rockfowl.

In Sialkot, Pakistan, the Fairtrade Premium partly paid for equipment that cleans up water. Now workers and local people can collect safe drinking water from taps outside two Fairtrade football factories.

11

A FAIRTRADE STORY: CHOCOLATE

Life for cocoa farmers is tough. Despite their hard work, they are often paid such a low price for their cocoa beans that they have to make tough choices about what they can afford to do. Fairtrade means that they have more security and can plan for the future.

Farming cocoa

Cocoa is a difficult crop to grow. The trees need shade, plenty of rain and warm weather. Farmers have to check their trees regularly as cocoa pods ripen throughout the year. Unpredictable weather, animal pests and plant diseases all pose big problems for cocoa farmers.

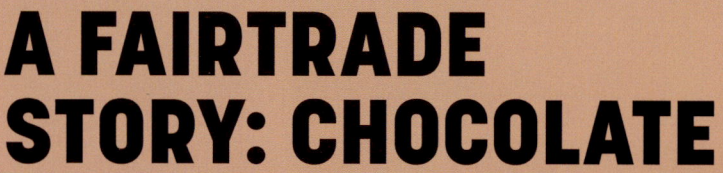

A cocoa pod, split open to reveal the raw beans.

Once cocoa pods have been harvested there is more work to be done. The cocoa beans are scooped out, fermented and dried out. All of this work is done by cocoa farmers and their workers, too.

To improve the flavour of cocoa beans, farmers pile them on leaves, then cover them with more leaves and allow them to ferment for about a week.

CHAPTER 2: A FAIRTRADE STORY: CHOCOLATE

Inside a chocolate factory

Unfair trade

When it comes to selling sacks of cocoa beans, most farmers have no control over the price they are paid because the price goes up and down on the world market. This makes it very difficult to plan for the future, improve land and stay out of poverty. The lack of money can lead to unsafe working conditions and the use of child labourers, who are cheaper than adults.

Most cocoa farmers receive a low price for their beans because the buyers have all the power. They want to pay a low price in order to cover their costs, and to make a profit. In turn, chocolate companies, shops and supermarkets have their own costs, including wages, machinery and transport costs, but still want to make as much profit as they can.

Fair or not?

Obviously everyone in the chocolate supply chain needs to make money. BUT the fact remains that even though there would be no chocolate bars without cocoa farmers, they only receive about 6 per cent of the money you pay for a chocolate bar. Does that seem fair to you?

The role of Fairtrade

When cocoa farmers sell their beans for at least the Fairtrade Minimum Price, they can improve life for themselves and their families.
- They can plan ahead.
- They can work together to improve their land with advice and training from their Fairtrade co-operative.
- They can share in the benefits from the Fairtrade Premium (see pages 9 and 11).

Sadly, most cocoa farmers do not sell their beans on Fairtrade terms. You can help increase the demand for Fairtrade cocoa beans by always buying Fairtrade chocolate.

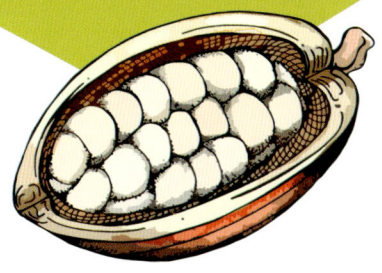

FOREST-FRIENDLY COCOA FARMING

For some of the cocoa farmers who live around the edge of the Gola rainforest in Sierra Leone, life has improved since their Fairtrade co-operative, Ngoleagorbu Cocoa Farmers' Union, was Fairtrade certified in 2019. The co-operative helps the farmers to earn more from their farms without damaging the rainforest and the animals that live there.

Lucia and her family belong to the Ngoleagorbu Cocoa Farmers' Union. They farm on the edge of the Gola rainforest, home to rare birds and butterflies.

Growing cocoa beans

The farmers plant cocoa trees in shady spots on the edge of the rainforest. Training from the co-operative means they now grow other crops too, so that they have something to eat or sell if the cocoa crop is damaged. Farmers are also learning how to control pests and diseases without pesticides.

Lucia holds a ripe cocoa pod.

CHAPTER 2: A FAIRTRADE STORY: CHOCOLATE

Harvesting

When the cocoa pods turn yellow or red, they are ripe. The farmers cut them down, collect them and take them back to their villages. Crack – they split the pods open to scoop the white, slimy cocoa beans into baskets and cover them with a leaf.

Fermenting helps cocoa beans develop their chocolatey flavour!

Drying

Next the farmers and their families spread the beans out onto drying tables built by the co-operative. The hot sun beats down on the beans for between six and ten days. When they are dry, each farmer fills a sack with their own beans.

Lucia's husband Sidie tips the fermented cocoa beans onto a drying table.

Sold!

It is time to sell the beans. Sidie takes his family's sack of beans to be weighed. The farmers are paid at least the Fairtrade Minimum Price for their beans. Now, the cocoa beans travel to the nearest city and on to Europe where they are made into chocolate.

Sidie watches to see how much his beans weigh.

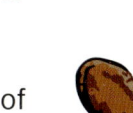

Protecting the forest

Ngoleagorbu cocoa farmers have learnt how to farm in a forest-friendly way so that they can meet Fairtrade Standards (see page 9). These include:

- growing their cocoa trees in the shade of rainforest trees
- farming organically
- learning new skills that result in better harvests
- not hunting or fishing in the rainforest
- not cutting down the rainforest
- scaring away chimpanzees, rather than killing them.

This way of farming cocoa is good for the planet and good for the farmers and their families. It can help them to move out of poverty and keep children in school.

Amie is Sidie's mother. She scares away chimpanzees by beating a drum so that they do not eat the family's precious cocoa beans.

Gbassay is the son of Lucia and Sidie and is Amie's grandson. The Fairtrade Premium helps pay his school fees and buys uniform, books and other equipment.

Using the Fairtrade Premium

The farmers meet together to decide how to use their Fairtrade Premium. Everyone has a voice. They plan to use the money to build water standpipes and two public toilets in each village, and continue to give money to families to support schoolchildren.

BAKE FAIRTRADE CHOCOLATE CHIP COOKIES

Here is a recipe to make delicious Fairtrade chocolate chip cookies. Don't forget to look for the FAIRTRADE Mark when you are shopping for ingredients.

Ingredients

110 g butter
200 g Fairtrade brown sugar
1 egg
210 g flour
1/2 teaspoon baking powder
150 g Fairtrade chocolate, broken into small bits
1 teaspoon Fairtrade vanilla extract

1. Take the butter out of the fridge an hour before you begin and chop it into pieces in a mixing bowl. Leave it to soften.

2. Use an electric mixer to mix the butter and sugar together. You can also do this by hand using a spoon.

3. Mix in the egg and vanilla extract.

4. Use a spoon to stir in the flour and baking powder.

5. Add the Fairtrade chocolate pieces.

6. Grease a baking sheet with butter. Drop dessertspoons of the mixture onto the baking sheet, leaving a little space between each cookie.

7. Bake for 15 minutes at 150 degrees C/ 300 degrees F/Gas 2.

8. Enjoy!

Ask an adult to switch on the oven and put the cookies inside – and take them out again. Don't forget to tidy up afterwards!

A FAIRTRADE STORY: BANANAS

Bananas were first transported from the tropics to the USA and Europe over 150 years ago. Today, it is very hard for small-scale banana farmers to compete with large banana plantations, which often receive new tools and technologies from the companies that buy their bananas. Fairtrade works with banana farmers to gain more control.

Meet Foncho

Foncho Cantillo is a banana farmer in Colombia, South America. He belongs to Coobafrio, a Fairtrade co-operative set up in the late 1990s. The farmers sell two-thirds of their bananas on Fairtrade terms.

Foncho Cantillo

Flowering and growing

Foncho works hard on his small banana farm, caring for his banana plants and making sure they have enough water and fertiliser. It takes about nine months to a year for each banana plant to flower, after which bunches of bananas start to form. There are about 50 bananas in each bunch.

Foncho protects them from pests by tying a plastic bag over each bunch.

CHAPTER 3: A FAIRTRADE STORY: BANANAS

Washing and packing

Foncho cuts down the bananas when they are still green and unripe. He carries them to the washing and packing room owned by Coobafrio. Here, the workers wash the bananas and cut them into smaller bunches. They stick a FAIRTRADE Mark sticker onto each bunch.

Workers in the packing house. Each co-operative has its own FLO-ID (see sticker, left).

Time for transport

Workers pack the Fairtrade bananas into boxes. A lorry driver comes to collect the boxes of bananas and transport them to the port, from where the bananas will travel to Europe by ship.

Ripening

The Fairtrade banana buyer arranges for a lorry driver to collect the boxes of bananas from the port and take them to a ripening room, where the bananas change from green to yellow as they ripen. When they are ready to eat, the bananas are sold to shops, supermarkets, restaurants and schools all around the world.

Foncho and Fairtrade

Now that Foncho is able to sell most of his bananas on Fairtrade terms, he can live a better life and plan for the future. He is saving money for when bad weather or pests destroy part of his crop. He can feed his family and improve his farm, and he has been able to pay for his children's education.

Being heard

As a member of Coobafrio, Foncho has a say in how the Fairtrade Premium is spent each year. The co-operative is spending money in many ways, including digging and clearing drains, improving the banana packing houses, helping farmers pay school fees and improving the lives of old people.

Keeping it green

Importantly, as Fairtrade producers, Coobafrio are also taking better care of the planet. The farmers are planting trees, using less pesticide and taking care to collect up and recycle the plastic they use to protect their bananas.

CHAPTER 3: A FAIRTRADE STORY: BANANAS

FAIRTRADE BANANA CAKE

Here is a recipe for a tasty Fairtrade banana cake to bake and enjoy.

Ingredients

- 1 ripe Fairtrade banana
- 125 g self-raising flour (plain or wholemeal)
- 100 g soft butter
- 100 g Fairtrade brown sugar
- 1/2 teaspoon Fairtrade vanilla extract
- 1 free-range egg

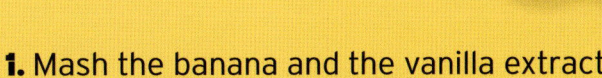

1. Mash the banana and the vanilla extract together in a bowl, using a fork.

2. Take another bowl and beat the butter and sugar together with an electric mixer or with a fork. Beat the egg into the mixture.

3. Add the banana and vanilla mix to the butter/sugar mix and beat again.

4. Stir in the flour.

5. Line a 500 g loaf tin with a paper liner, or with greaseproof paper.

6. Scrape the cake mixture into the loaf tin and bake for 40 minutes at 190 degrees C/375 degrees F/Gas 5.

Ask an adult to switch on the oven and put the cake inside – and take it out again. Don't forget to tidy up afterwards!

A FAIRTRADE STORY: COFFEE

Coffee is made from roasted coffee beans, the fruit of coffee trees. Some people grow rich from selling coffee but it usually isn't the farmers. This is because the price they are paid for their coffee beans goes up and down, while the cost of growing coffee keeps rising.

Coffee plants growing in Peru

Weather challenges

Coffee plants are small trees or shrubs with green, waxy leaves. They grow in countries where it is not too hot, but rains often. Climate change is making life difficult for coffee farmers. Rain is often not falling when the plants need it, but sometimes it can rain so much that soil is washed away and plant diseases spread.

Leaf rust is caused by fungi that spread in wet weather, attacking the leaves of coffee trees. Over time, it can kill them.

Co-operatives

Thousands of coffee farmers belong to Fairtrade co-operatives. Over the years, many of these coffee co-operatives have used the Fairtrade Premium to help pay for education and training.

CHAPTER 4: A FAIRTRADE STORY: COFFEE

Norandino

Norandino is a Fairtrade coffee co-operative in Peru. It represents about 7,000 small-scale farmers. Since it was set up in 1993, the farmers have used some of the Fairtrade Premium to pay for their children, including Hugo Guerrero (below, far left) to go to school and further education. Now Hugo is passing on what he has learnt.

Hugo Guerrero with his family on their farm. His father was a founding member of Norandino.

Giving back

Hugo shows other farmers how to make organic fertiliser and protect the soil during droughts. Following his advice, farmers are starting to grow their coffee plants on higher land, where it is cooler, using the lower land for other crops, such as cocoa and sugar cane. These other crops will also give the farmers something to sell if the coffee crop fails.

A Norandino coffee producer harvests ripe coffee fruits, called cherries.

The coffee trail

Training provided by Fairtrade is helping farmers across the world to carry on growing coffee. Follow the trail to see how coffee is grown.

1. Farmers plant coffee seedlings, which grow into trees. Farmers check the trees to make sure they have enough water and are not being attacked by insect pests or diseases.

2. After three or four years the trees flower. Insects pollinate the flowers so that they can grow coffee cherries.

3. The farmers handpick ripe, red coffee cherries and carry them back to the farm. Each cherry contains two seeds – the coffee beans.

4. Fairtrade co-operatives usually have the equipment to process the coffee beans. This may include cleaning, pulping, fermenting and drying the beans.

5. The co-operative sells sacks of coffee beans to a roaster who will pay at least the Fairtrade Minimum Price and the Fairtrade Premium.

Green coffee beans

BAKE MOCHA CHOC FAIRY CAKES

Use Fairtrade coffee to make the strong coffee needed for the icing on these fairy cakes.

Ingredients

For the fairy cakes:
100 g soft butter
100 g Fairtrade sugar
100 g self-raising flour
30 g Fairtrade cocoa powder
2 free-range eggs

For the icing:
60 g butter
170 g icing sugar
50 g Fairtrade cocoa powder
1 tablespoon Fairtrade instant coffee (make it strong by using two teaspoons of coffee powder to 1 tablespoon of hot water)
1 tablespoon milk

1. Place all the ingredients for the cakes in a large mixing bowl and beat, using a hand mixer, until the mixture turns creamy and pale.

2. Place a paper fairy cake case in each hole of a 12-hole bun tin.

3. Scrape a dessertspoon of mixture into each paper case.

4. Bake for 15 minutes at 180 degrees C/350 degrees F/Gas 4.

5. Leave to cool.

6. Make the mocha icing by melting the butter in a small pan. Remove from the heat and stir in the icing sugar, cocoa powder and enough instant coffee to make it smooth enough to spread onto your cakes. If the mixture is too stiff, add a drop of milk.

7. Share out the icing across your fairy cakes.

Ask an adult to switch on the oven and put the cakes inside – and take them out again. Don't forget to tidy up afterwards!

A FAIRTRADE STORY: TEA

Tea is made by adding boiling water to tea leaves or a teabag and leaving them to brew in a teapot or cup. Tea leaves travel along a supply chain that starts with the farmers who tend the tea bushes, and ends with tea being sold in shops.

Bush to teacup

Tea leaves grow on bushes in countries such as India, China, Kenya and Sri Lanka. Tea growers plant tea bushes in good soil on small farms and huge ones. These are called plantations, tea estates or tea gardens and they employ a lot of people.

A tea estate in India

Pluckers at work on the Welbeck Estate in India

Harvest time

It takes two or more years before the tea bush is ready for its first harvest. Farmers or workers weed, fertilise and prune the bushes. On the Fairtrade Welbeck Estate in the Nilgiri Hills, India, workers pluck two or three leaves and a bud from the top of each tea bush and place them in a basket.

CHAPTER 5: A FAIRTRADE STORY: TEA

Rolling, drying and bagging

Now rolling machines twist and turn the leaves. The leaves are separated into different sizes and oxidised. This means they are left outside to develop more flavour. After Fairtrade tea leaves have dried out some more, they are sold at Fairtrade prices to tea buyers. They will transport the tea leaves to a factory where they will be poured into packets or sealed inside teabags. The tea is then transported to shops and supermarkets around the world.

Rolling machines in a tea factory in Sri Lanka

Withering

When the basket is full, the pluckers take it to a collection point. From here the tea leaves are taken to a factory on the estate where they are dried. This is called withering.

Withering at a tea factory in Sri Lanka

27

FAIRTRADE AND TEA

When it comes to selling the tea, producers are paid the Fairtrade Minimum Price. This allows them to plan ahead and feed their families. It also means the owners of tea estates can pay workers better wages, while the Fairtrade Premium can improve their lives in other ways.

The Welbeck Estate

The Welbeck Estate in India has met Fairtrade Standards since 1994. The estate has always run a school for the workers' children, but workers can now use some of the Fairtrade Premium to provide better school meals and pay for sports equipment. The fund pays for a bus to transport older children to schools further away. Some of the children will receive money to help them go to university.

Welbeck Estate workers line up at the start of another working day. The estate grows organic tea, which is much better for workers' health, as well as the planet.

CHAPTER 5: A FAIRTRADE STORY: TEA

Health

The estate runs a medical centre for its workers, but they use the Fairtrade Premium to help pay for things such as new equipment, an ambulance and vaccinations. When workers fall ill, medical bills soon mount up. The Premium helps workers pay these bills so that they can return to health without worrying about money.

The future

Money from the Premium fund has improved life for workers and their families on the Welbeck Estate. The Fairtrade Premium has enabled workers to plan for the future. They can invest in other ways of earning money, in addition to their pay from the tea estate, such as buying cows to have milk to sell.

A FAIRTRADE STORY: SUGAR

Sugar comes from two very different plants – sugar beet and sugar cane. Fairtrade sugar is made from sugar cane, a crop grown in hot countries near the equator. When you buy Fairtrade sugar you are making a difference to the lives of sugar farmers.

Cane sugar comes from tall grasses called sugar cane.

Sugar in Malawi

Kasinthula Cane Growers' Association is a Fairtrade sugar co-operative in Malawi. Most of the farmers own a small amount of land on which they grow sugar cane, as well as other crops to feed their families. This co-operative also supports people who work for the sugar cane farmers.

Planting

The farmers or workers dig a trench and plant short sections of sugar cane stalk. These will sprout two or three stalks each. The thirsty plants need to be weeded and watered. They grow and grow until they are about 6 m tall.

This farmer is laying sections of cane stalk into a trench in Zambia.

CHAPTER 6: A FAIRTRADE STORY: SUGAR

Harvesting

After 12-18 months, it is time to harvest the cane stalks. In many places, the green leaves are burnt off by starting a fire. This makes it easier to cut down the canes and carry them off to the collection point.

All of the Kasinthula sugar cane is sold to the Illovo sugar mill in Malawi, where the sugar is chopped and crushed to release the sugary juices. It goes through several stages until it looks like this:

Droughts in Malawi result in failed harvests across the country.

Climate crisis

Life can be tough for Malawi's sugar farmers, as the changing weather causes floods one month and droughts the next. The farmers' crops die and the soil washes away. Sometimes the farmers are left with nothing to sell to pay for food and other everyday needs.

Fairtrade Premium

There is no such thing as a Fairtrade Minimum Price for sugar, but the Kasinthula farmers in Malawi have used the Fairtrade Premium to meet the needs of their community. The Premium has paid for improvements to farms and bicycle ambulances, and for new boreholes which supply safe, clean drinking water. The farmers have also used the money to build a new primary school.

Communities in Malawi are gradually building more boreholes so that people can pump up clean drinking water.

CHAPTER 6: A FAIRTRADE STORY: SUGAR

BAKE FAIRTRADE BROWNIES

Brownies have a lot of sugar in them! Make it Fairtrade sugar and cut these into small pieces.

Ingredients

100 g Fairtrade white chocolate, broken into small chips

175 g unsalted butter

65 g Fairtrade cocoa powder

340 g Fairtrade caster sugar

2 medium free-range eggs

1 teaspoon Fairtrade vanilla extract (if you have it)

100 g plain flour

Pinch of salt

1. Take a saucepan that will be big enough to act as your mixing bowl. Melt the butter in the pan over a low heat and take it off the heat.

2. Place the saucepan safely on a kitchen surface and use a sieve to sift the cocoa powder into the butter.

3. Stir in the cocoa powder and the sugar.

4. Beat the eggs and vanilla extract with a fork and stir into the mixture.

5. Sift the flour into the pan and stir well. Add a pinch of salt and the white chocolate chips.

6. Line a 20 cm x 20 cm cake tin with baking parchment. Pour the mixture into the cake tin and bake for 30 minutes at 180 degrees C/350 degrees F/Gas 4.

7. Remove from the oven and allow to cool. Cut into pieces. Enjoy!

Ask an adult to switch on the oven and put the cakes inside – and take them out again. Don't forget to tidy up afterwards!

A FAIRTRADE STORY: COTTON

Are any of your clothes made of cotton? Cotton farmers are at the start of a long supply chain and are often paid very little for their crops. Fairtrade supports cotton farmers and workers to get a fairer deal.

Picking Fairtrade cotton in India

Fairtrade cotton

Most Fairtrade cotton is grown by small-scale farmers in West Africa and India. By paying them a fair price for their crops, farmers can plan for the future and move out of poverty. The farmers' co-operatives use the Fairtrade Premium to build schools, support schoolchildren, improve the land and train farmers and workers in how to reduce the use of pesticides or even grow organic cotton.

Follow the steps to see the work of Fairtrade cotton farmers in India.

1. The farmer ploughs the land, adds fertiliser and plants cotton seeds before the rainy season.

CHAPTER 7: A FAIRTRADE STORY: COTTON

4. This can be a dangerous time for the cotton crop. Insects like to eat cotton bolls, including the boll weevil (right). Fairtrade farmers control insect pests with organic pesticides or traps. These have to be paid for out of any profit made when they sell the cotton harvest.

3. The plants grow tall, as long as there is enough rain. Now the plants burst into flower. When the petals drop off, the cottonseed pods, or bolls, start to develop.

2. Two or three weeks later, small plants start growing.

35

5. The cotton bolls split open to reveal the fluffy white fibres that protect the cotton seeds. Cotton farmers, their families and other workers pick the cotton bolls. It is hard work in the hot sun.

6. The pickers pile up the raw cotton by the side of the field. Other workers collect the bundles of cotton and carry them to a collecting point.

7. Fairtrade farmers sell their cotton to a ginning mill and receive at least the Fairtrade Minimum Price. Here the cotton is being unloaded at the ginning mill where the threads will be separated from the seeds, ready to be spun into thread.

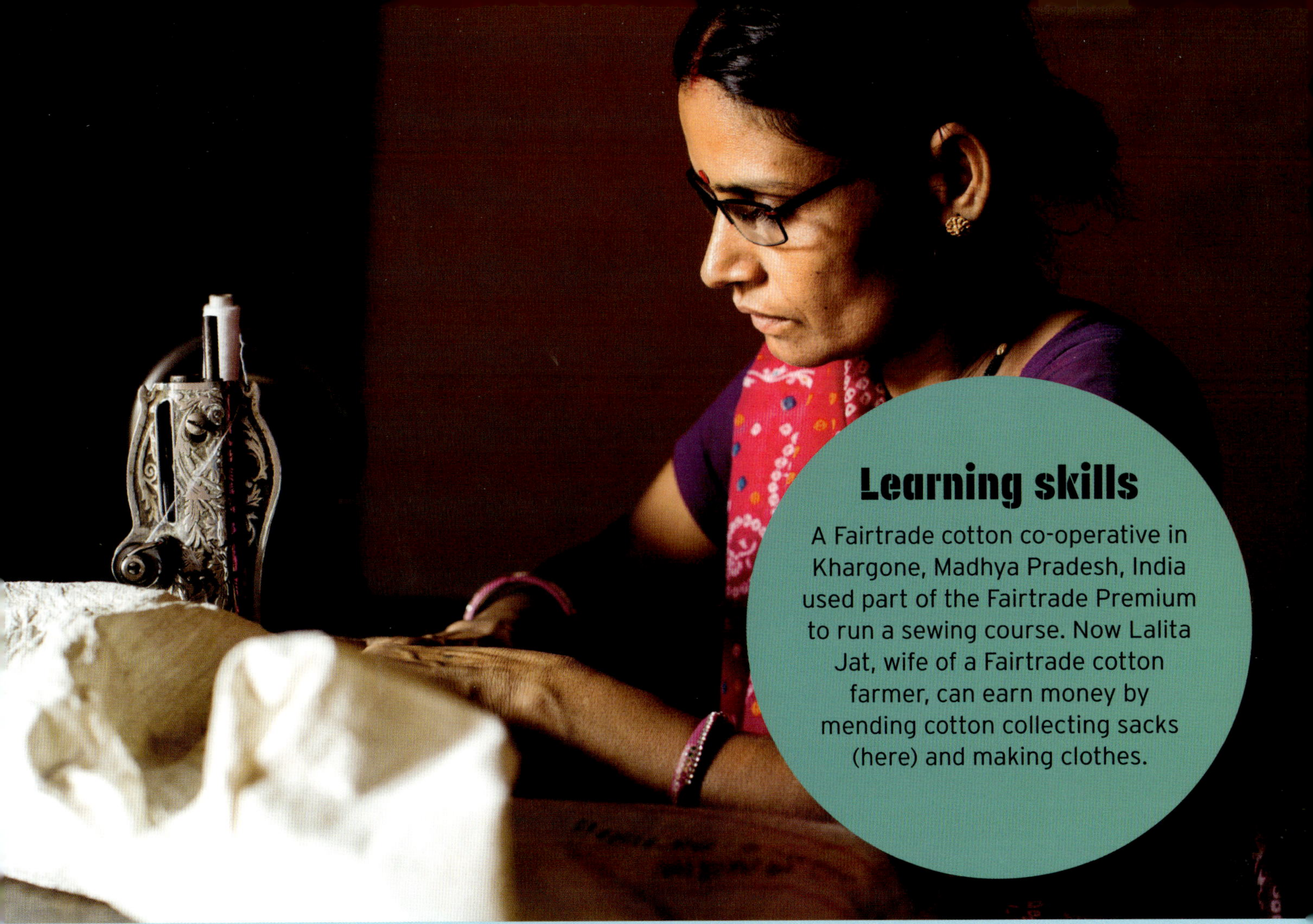

Learning skills

A Fairtrade cotton co-operative in Khargone, Madhya Pradesh, India used part of the Fairtrade Premium to run a sewing course. Now Lalita Jat, wife of a Fairtrade cotton farmer, can earn money by mending cotton collecting sacks (here) and making clothes.

FAIRTRADE marks

Look for the FAIRTRADE Mark on cotton clothes. It means the farmers were paid a fair price for their hard work in growing the cotton.

Fairtrade also supports workers who help to spin the cotton fibres into thread, weave it into fabric and make it into cotton clothes, bedlinen or other cotton things. Slowly, the Fairtrade Textile Production Mark standards are helping to improve the lives of these workers too.

MORE FAIRTRADE PRODUCTS

A football, a bunch of flowers, some nuts, a jar of honey. When you buy Fairtrade products such as these, you are making a difference to the lives of Fairtrade farmers and workers around the world.

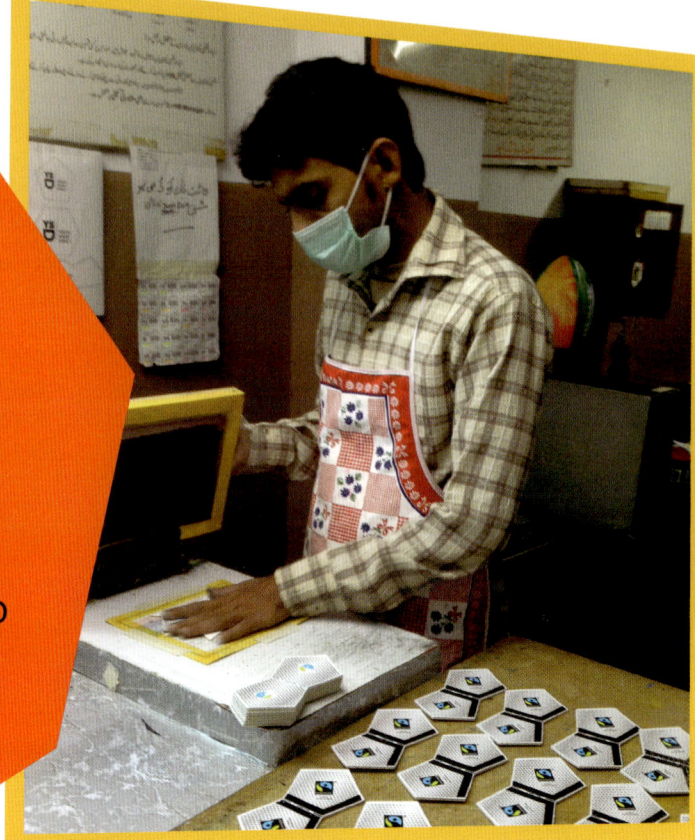

A worker at one of Bala Sport's Fairtrade football factories prints the FAIRTRADE Mark onto pieces that will become part of Fairtrade footballs.

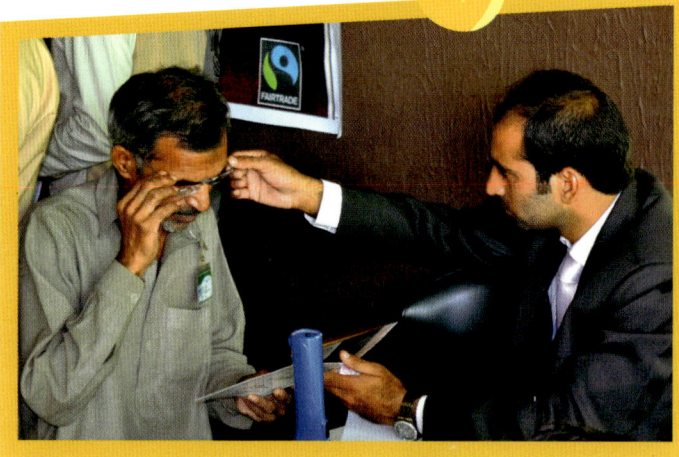

A Fairtrade worker receives a free eye test, paid for by the Fairtrade Premium. Workers also get help towards the cost of glasses.

Fair play

More than 70 per cent of the world's hand-stitched footballs are made in Sialkot in Pakistan. Here, lots of hexagon- and pentagon-shaped pieces are cut out, printed and stitched together by workers to make the balls. In the past, factories employed children, paid very low wages and made people work in unsafe conditions. In Fairtrade factories, workers are supported in several ways:
- the workers are paid a fair wage
- they work in safe factories
- their children do not work in the factories
- they receive the Fairtrade Premium, which they can choose to spend on things like free eye tests, transport and school books
- water treatment plants have taps outside the factories so that all in the area can collect clean drinking water (see page 11).

CHAPTER 8: MORE FAIRTRADE PRODUCTS

Can a bunch of flowers make a difference?

Yes! Next time you are out shopping for a bunch of flowers as a gift, look for the FAIRTRADE Mark on the label. That way you'll know that you are supporting the people who grew and picked the flowers, and the planet. To get the FAIRTRADE Mark, flower growers have to:

- use less pesticides, which is safer for workers and wildlife
- reuse and recycle water and aim to reduce waste
- pay workers a fair wage
- ensure workers have safe working conditions
- give everyone a say in how the Fairtrade Premium is spent. This might be for school desks or toilets, vaccinations, training courses or sports equipment for workers to use.

Maru Mueni Musyoki works at Panda Flowers, a fairtrade farm in Kenya. The workers' co-operative makes sure that men and women are treated fairly and equally.

39

What about ice cream?

Look for the FAIRTRADE Mark on vanilla ice cream. It means that vanilla growers were paid a fair price for growing and harvesting the plant. The vanilla flavour comes from the dried seed pods of the plant.

Vanilla pods before harvest

Spice farmers

The Small Organic Farmers' Association (SOFA) is a Sri Lankan co-operative of tea and spice farmers. Using the Fairtrade Premium, they have set up a fund so that members can borrow money to start businesses or buy farm equipment.

Root ginger, a spice used in many recipes, comes from the root of the ginger plant. It is one of the crops grown by SOFA co-operative members.

CHAPTER 8: MORE FAIRTRADE PRODUCTS

Almonds

A peanut farmer in Malawi gathers his crops.

Go nuts for Fairtrade!

If you like nuts, buy Fairtrade peanuts, cashews and almonds. Did you know that peanuts grow under the ground? In Malawi, the Mchinji Area Smallholder Farmers' Association has been helping a growing number of small-scale farmers improve their livelihoods through Fairtrade. Over 2,000 farmers belong to the association, which buys all of the peanuts they grow, allowing them to plan for the future.

The farmers have used the Fairtrade Premium to build a guardian shelter at the local hospital. This provides basic accommodation for people who have come to visit their relatives at the hospital, which is needed because they have often travelled a long way from their homes. They have also used the Premium fund to pay off debts and build warehouses in some villages.

Look for the FAIRTRADE Mark

As well as all the foods you've read about already, there are also Fairtrade producers gathering honey, pressing olives and growing rice, dates, pineapples and avocados. They also farm grapes to make wine.

Buy Fairtrade honey to support Fairtrade beekeepers.

SUPPORT FAIRTRADE

Since 1997, Fairtrade Fortnight has helped to bring attention to the aims of the Fairtrade movement. It is held every year in countries including the UK, Australia, New Zealand and Canada. If you live in an area where there are no Fairtrade Fortnight events, see if you can get the idea to catch on.

What happens?

People in schools, places of worship, universities, supermarkets and charity shops plan events such as Fairtrade fairs, tasting events, bake sales and fashion shows. What could your family, school, club or place of worship do to draw attention to the importance of Fairtrade?

Fairtrade bake sale

How about organising a bake sale? All through this book there are recipes which use Fairtrade ingredients to make tasty baked goods. Make posters to advertise your bake sale to put up on noticeboards and online sites. Ask your parents or carers if they could serve Fairtrade tea or coffee, and remember to donate the money you make to a Fairtrade organisation. A trusted adult can help you do this.

CHAPTER 9: SUPPORT FAIRTRADE

Fairtrade sports tournament

Ask your school, sports club or youth group whether you can organise a Fairtrade football or rugby tournament together to raise awareness of Fairtrade sports balls. The competition can take whatever form you decide on, but the balls all need to be Fairtrade.

Hear from a Fairtrade producer

Contact your local Fairtrade organisation to see if they can arrange for a Fairtrade farmer or worker to come to your school and give a talk.

Fairtrade assembly

Hold a Fairtrade assembly to bring attention to the ideas behind Fairtrade. There are several ready-to-go presentations on Fairtrade websites. Or you could plan your own Fairtrade assembly with friends. Use books and online resources to research and plan the presentation. You could even ask your teacher whether your school could become a Fairtrade School – see page 47 for how to do this.

QUESTIONS AND ANSWERS

Now that you've learnt about Fairtrade, tell all your friends and family about it too. It is good to be prepared if people ask you questions. These questions and answers might help.

Q: Why are low wages still a problem for Fairtrade farmers?

A: The number of people buying Fairtrade goods is still very low. Most small producers are forced to take the prices set by their buyers and have no power to negotiate. Even those who are Fairtrade-certified rarely sell all their produce for a Fairtrade price and are still forced to sell the rest for whatever price they can get.

Q: Shouldn't I buy local foods rather than Fairtrade foods grown far away?

A: It is true that many Fairtrade foods are grown a long way away as that is where those crops grow well. But are you prepared to give up bananas, olives, mangoes, coffee, chocolate and cotton clothes, or would you rather support those producers to have better lives by buying their Fairtrade goods? You can support local farmers and producers too.

Q: Why are Fairtrade foods more expensive?

A: Actually, Fairtrade and non-Fairtrade foods are often very similar in price. Shops and supermarkets can choose to make slightly less money for themselves in order to make Fairtrade food the same price. Look for own-brand Fairtrade products in shops and supermarkets.

Q: Where can I buy Fairtrade products?

A: Most supermarkets stock Fairtrade food products, while some cafes and restaurants serve Fairtrade drinks and foods. Look out for the FAIRTRADE Mark on the packaging or the menu. For Fairtrade clothing or household items, use a reliable search engine to do an online search and go from there. Also remember to look out for Fairtrade labels or logos when you are in shops.

Q: How can I trust that all parts of a Fairtrade supply chain are fair?

A: An independent company called Flo Cert carries out checks along the supply chain to make sure producers and workers keep to Fairtrade Standards. They cannot be everywhere at once, but they do their best.

Q: Why should I buy Fairtrade goods?

A: Because that means the Fairtrade producer or worker was paid a fair amount for their work and can plan for the future. The Fairtrade movement continues to work towards workers and producers having a decent standard of living. Fairtrade Standards also help people care for our planet.

GLOSSARY

agent Someone who buys products from producers to sell on to others.

axe head The sharp, cutting blade of an axe.

basic needs The things that are necessary for survival such as food, shelter, clothes, warmth and clean drinking water.

boll weevil A beetle that damages cotton plants by eating cotton flowers and buds.

buyer In a supply chain, the person who assesses the quality of a good or service, and buys it, to sell on to a wholesaler or whoever is on the next step of the supply chain.

child labourer A child who works on a farm or in a factory, often illegally.

climate change The change in the normal weather patterns of planet Earth.

community A group of people who live in a particular area, such as part of a town or a village, or an online community of people with the same interests or concerns.

consumer Someone who buys food or clothes, for instance, for their own use or that of their family.

co-operative In this book, a group of farmers who join together to work for better prices for their crops and a better life for the members of the co-operative and their families.

crop A plant grown in large quantities for food, such as wheat, sugar, rice or apples.

environment The natural world, in which all plants and animals, including people, live.

equator The imaginary line around the widest part of planet Earth, at an equal distance from the North and South Poles.

export To sell goods to another business in a different country.

fair Treating people equally.

fair price Paying a producer fairly for what they have grown or made. It should be enough to cover a person's basic needs and the costs of production.

fair trade All the people and organisations, including Fairtrade International, that are working to make trade fair by offering a different way of doing business.

Fairtrade-certified A product that can carry the FAIRTRADE Mark because it has met Fairtrade Standards (see below).

Fairtrade Minimum Price Fairtrade producers receive a price for their harvest/goods that goes up and down on the world market, but the Fairtrade price paid by the buyer never goes below an agreed Fairtrade Minimum Price. This should be enough to cover a producer's basic needs (see left) and the cost of producing the crop or goods.

Fairtrade Premium The top-up price paid to a co-operative (per sack or other arrangement) which the co-operative must spend on community projects or invest in their businesses by common agreement, after meeting with members of the co-operative.

Fairtrade Standards The requirements which producers must meet in order to have their products Fairtrade-certified. They include rules such as not harming the environment, not employing children and giving an equal voice to men and women in the co-operative.

ferment In cocoa beans, allowing yeast to start breaking them down, changing the flavour.

fertiliser Something added to soil to make plants grow better.

ginning mill The place where cotton seeds are separated from cotton fibres by machines.

global The whole world.

goods Things that are grown or made to be sold.

harvest The amount of crop that has been grown and gathered.

import A business that buys goods produced in another country and brings them across the sea, or by land, to sell them on to customers.

investment Putting money into something, such as a farm or business, in the hope that it will improve the farm or business.

loan An amount of money that is lent to a person or organisation, but which must be paid back.

manufacturer A factory or organisation that makes (manufactures) goods in large quantities.

organic A type of farming where the grower does not use artificial pesticides or fertilisers.

pesticide A chemical sprayed onto crops or plants to kill pests, especially insects.

plantation A large area of land where crops such as tea, coffee, sugar or tea are grown.

pollinate To move pollen to the female part of a flower, leading to fertilisation.

poverty Being very poor, with not enough money for basic needs such as food, shelter and clothes.

prehistoric The time in history before people started writing down information.

producer A farmer who grows crops to sell, such as cotton, mangoes or bananas. A small-scale producer is a farmer who only has a small plot of land.

prune To cut off some branches from a tree or plant so that it will grow back stronger or better.

rainforest A thick forest in tropical areas (near the equator) where it rains a lot.

rainy season The time of the year when most of a country's rain falls over the course of a few days, weeks or months.

service industry Someone who works to provide a service, such as a builder, teacher, banker or insurance broker.

standard of living The amount of comfort, or wealth, that a person or a group of people experience.

standpipe A water pipe or tap, connected to a well, groundwater or other water supply.

sugar cane A tall plant with thick stems, from which sugar is made.

supply chain Several stages involving people and activities that move a product (say the cocoa beans used to make a chocolate bar) from where it is grown or made, to where it is sold to a consumer.

tea estate A large area of land owned by one person or family, where tea is the main crop.

trade Buying and selling.

vs. Short for 'versus', meaning 'compared to'.

wholesaler A person or a company that buys goods in large quantities to sell on to other companies, shops or people.

world market The trading of goods or services produced in one country to people of other countries.

Further information

Find out how to become a Fairtrade School here: *https://schools.fairtrade.org.uk/fairtrade-schools-awards/*

Access Fairtrade Schools resources here: *https://schools.fairtrade.org.uk/teaching-resources/#page-1include Fairtrade Foundation*

Find out more about how cocoa beans turn into Divine chocolate bars here: *www.divinechocolate.com/bean-to-bar*

Find out more about how Fairtrade and the RSPB are helping to save the wildlife of the Gola rainforest here: *www.rspb.org.uk/about-the-rspb/at-home-and-abroad/international/tropical-forests/greater-gola/*

*Every effort has been made by the Publishers to ensure that the websites in this book are suitable for children, that they are of the highest educational value, and that they contain no inappropriate or offensive material. However, because of **the nature of the Internet, it is impossible to guarantee that the contents of these sites will not be altered. We strongly advise that internet access is supervised by a responsible adult.***

INDEX

chains, supply 5, 13, 18-19, 26, 34, 45

climate change 22, 32

co-operatives, Fairtrade
- banana co-operatives 18-20
- cocoa co-operatives 8-10, 12-16, 43
- coffee co-operatives 22-24
- Coobafrio 18-20
- cotton co-operatives 34-37
- flower-growers co-operatives 39
- football factory workers' co-operative 11, 38, 43
- Kasinthula Cane Growers' Association 30-32
- Kuapa Kokoo 8-9
- Mchinji Area Smallholder Farmers' Association 41
- Ngoleagorbu Cocoa Farmers' Union 14-16
- Norandino 23
- Small Organic Farmers' Association (SOFA) 40
- sugar co-operatives 30-32
- tea co-operatives 26-29, 40
- vanilla farmer co-operative 40
- Welbeck Estate Fairtrade workers' co-operative 26-29

environment, protecting the 9-11, 14-16, 20, 23, 28, 34-35, 39, 45

Fairtrade
- Fairtrade Fortnight 42-43
- FAIRTRADE Mark 10-11, 17, 19, 37-41, 45
- Fairtrade Minimum Price 9, 11, 13, 15, 24, 27-28, 32, 36, 44
- Fairtrade movement 8-11, 42-45
- Fairtrade Premium 9, 11, 13, 16, 20, 22-24, 28-29, 32, 34, 37-41
- Fairtrade Standards 8-10, 16, 28, 45

farmers
- banana 18-20
- cocoa 8-10, 12-16, 23
- coffee 22-24
- cotton 34-37
- flowers 39
- honey 41
- mangoes 5
- nut 41
- spices 40
- sugar cane 10, 23, 30-33
- tea 26-29, 40
- vanilla 40

Gola rainforest 11, 14-16

poverty 7-8, 10, 13, 16, 34

producers 6-11, 42-45 see also farmers
- basic needs 7
- football factory workers 11, 38, 43
- small-scale producers 6-7
- textile production workers 37

recipes
- banana cake 21
- brownies 33
- chocolate chip cookies 17
- mocha choc fairy cakes 25

services 4-5

trade, definition of 4-5
- prehistoric 4